Doodle Ar

Guinea Pigs

Annette Rand

www.doodleartist.co.uk

Contents

2 copies of each picture

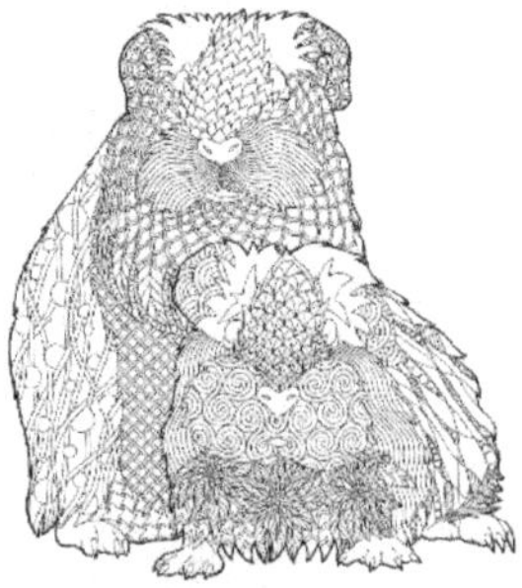
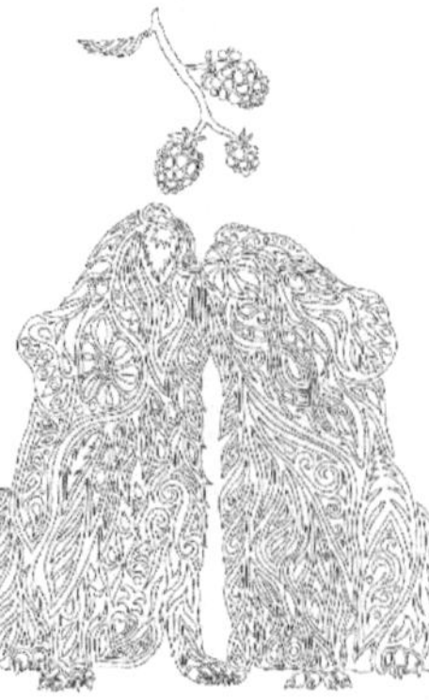

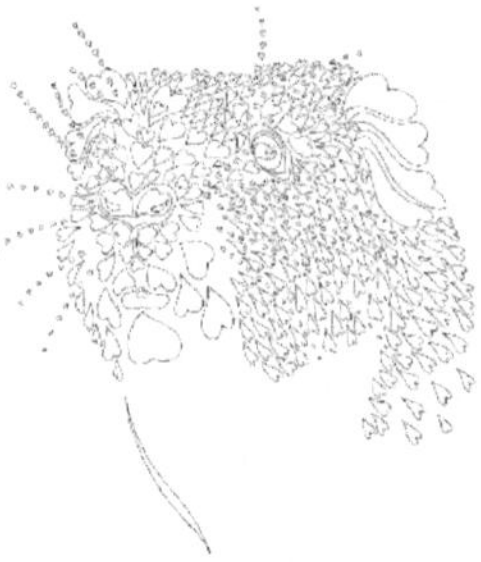
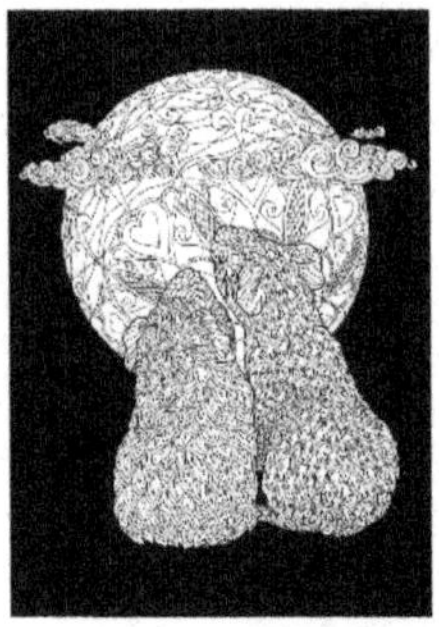
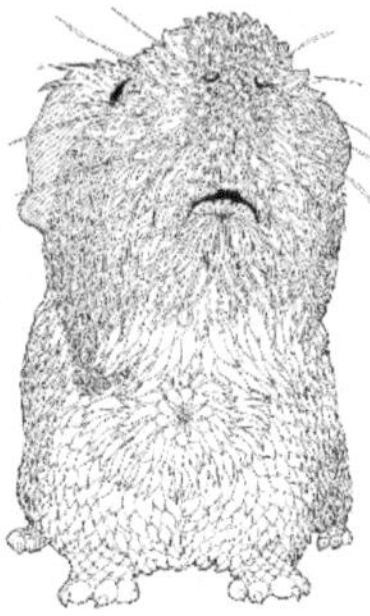

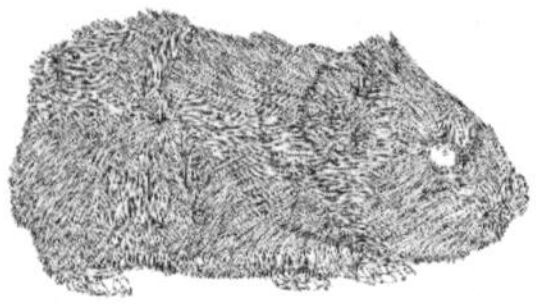

ISBN-13: 978-1539162339

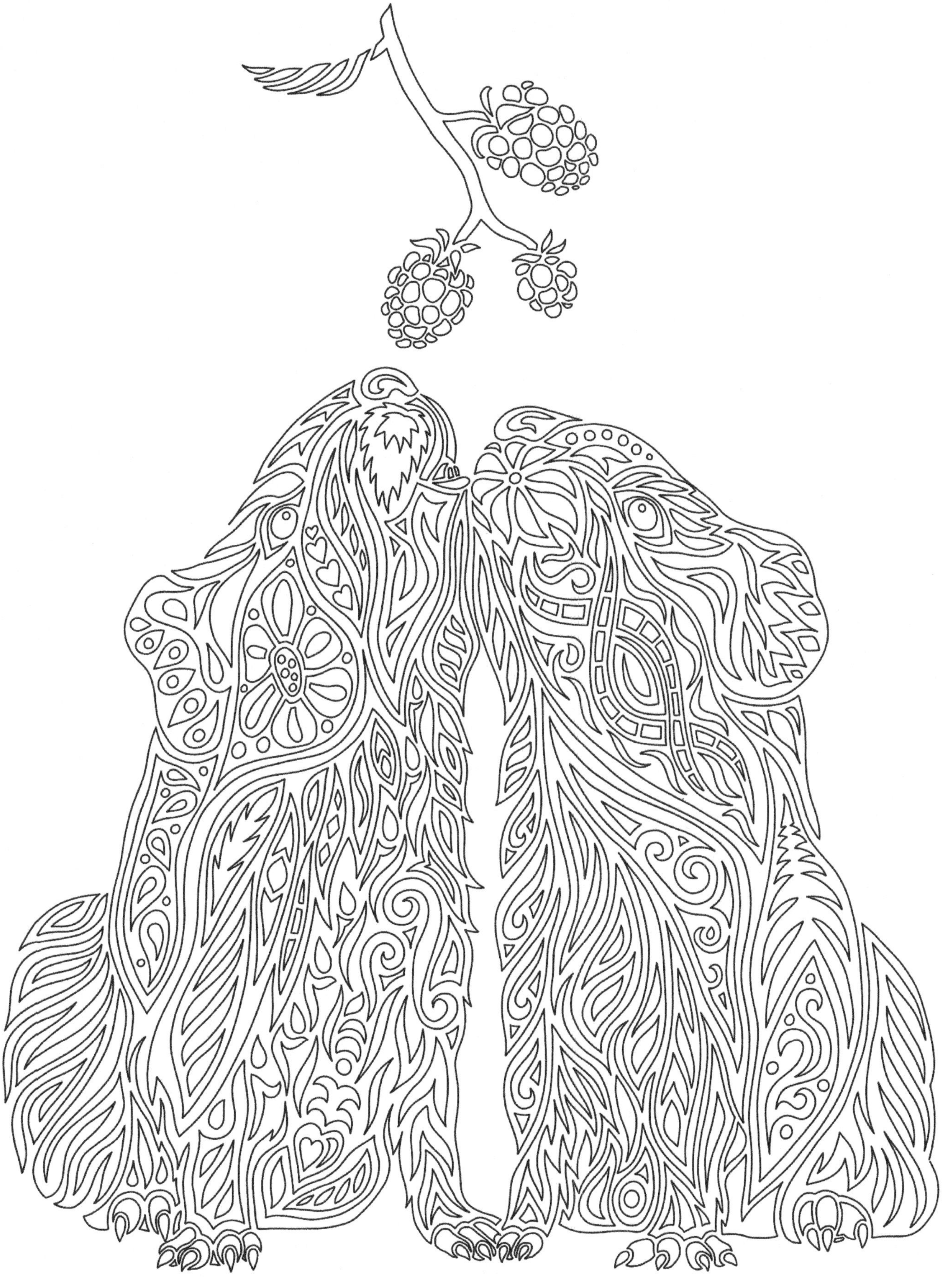

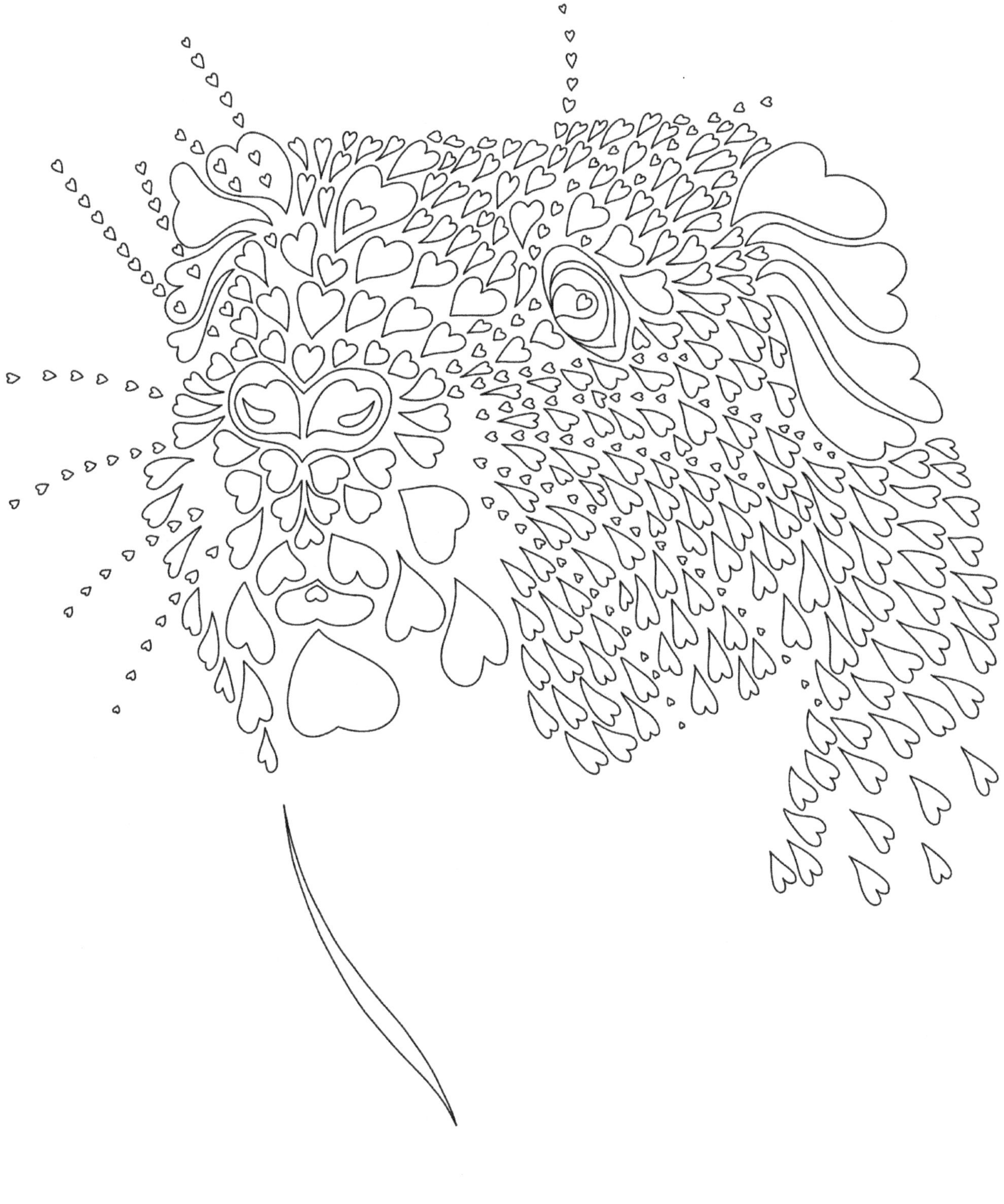

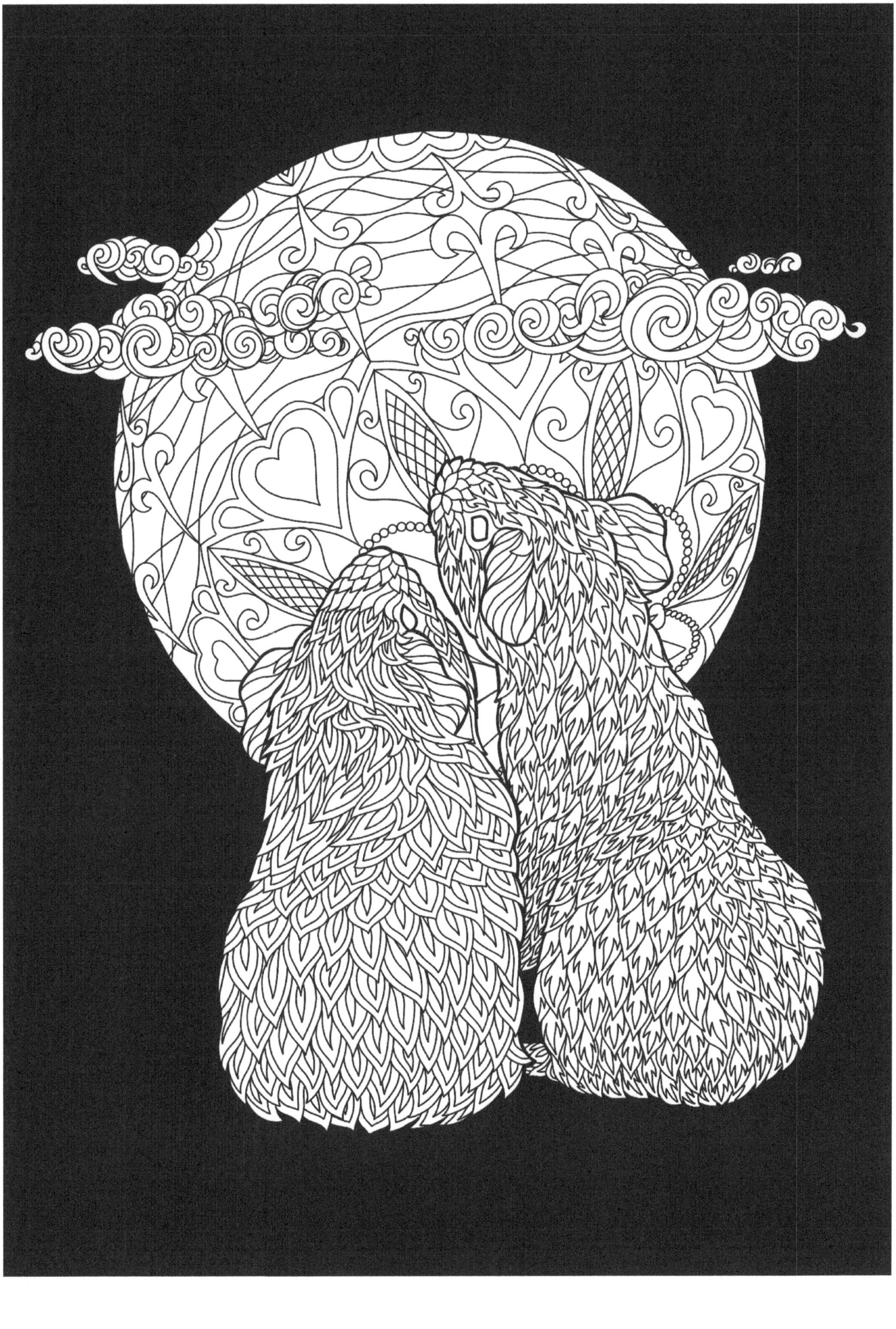

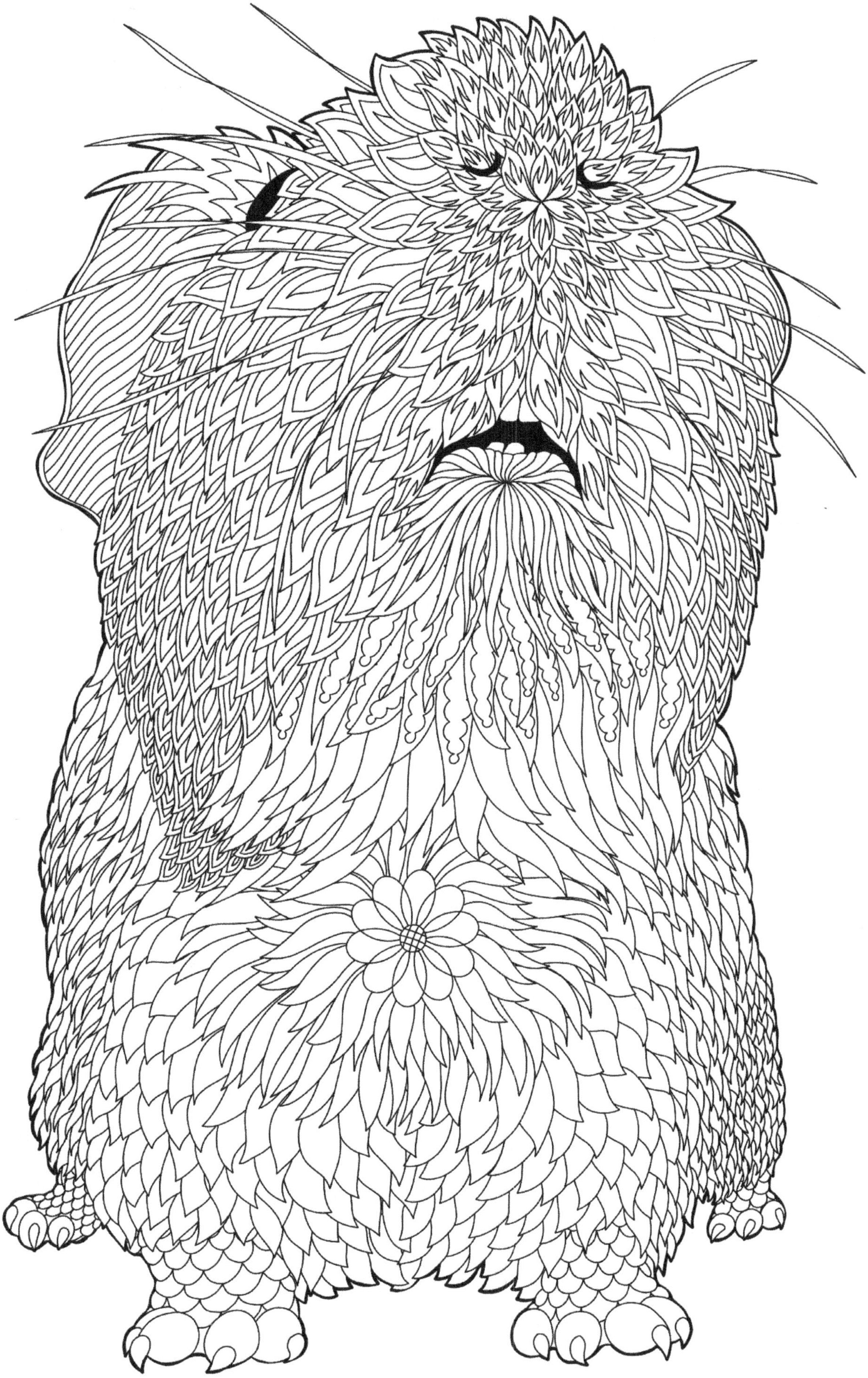

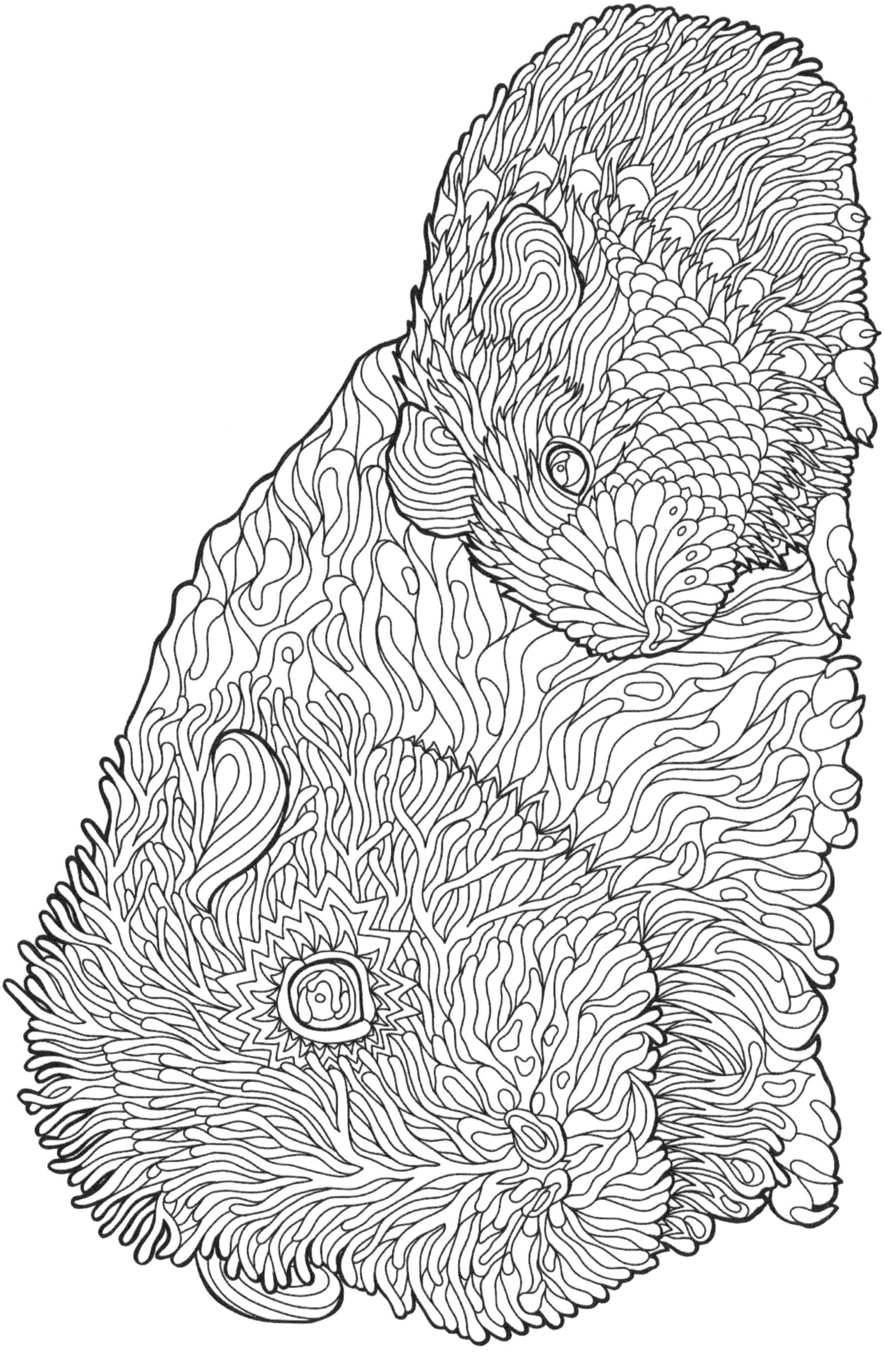

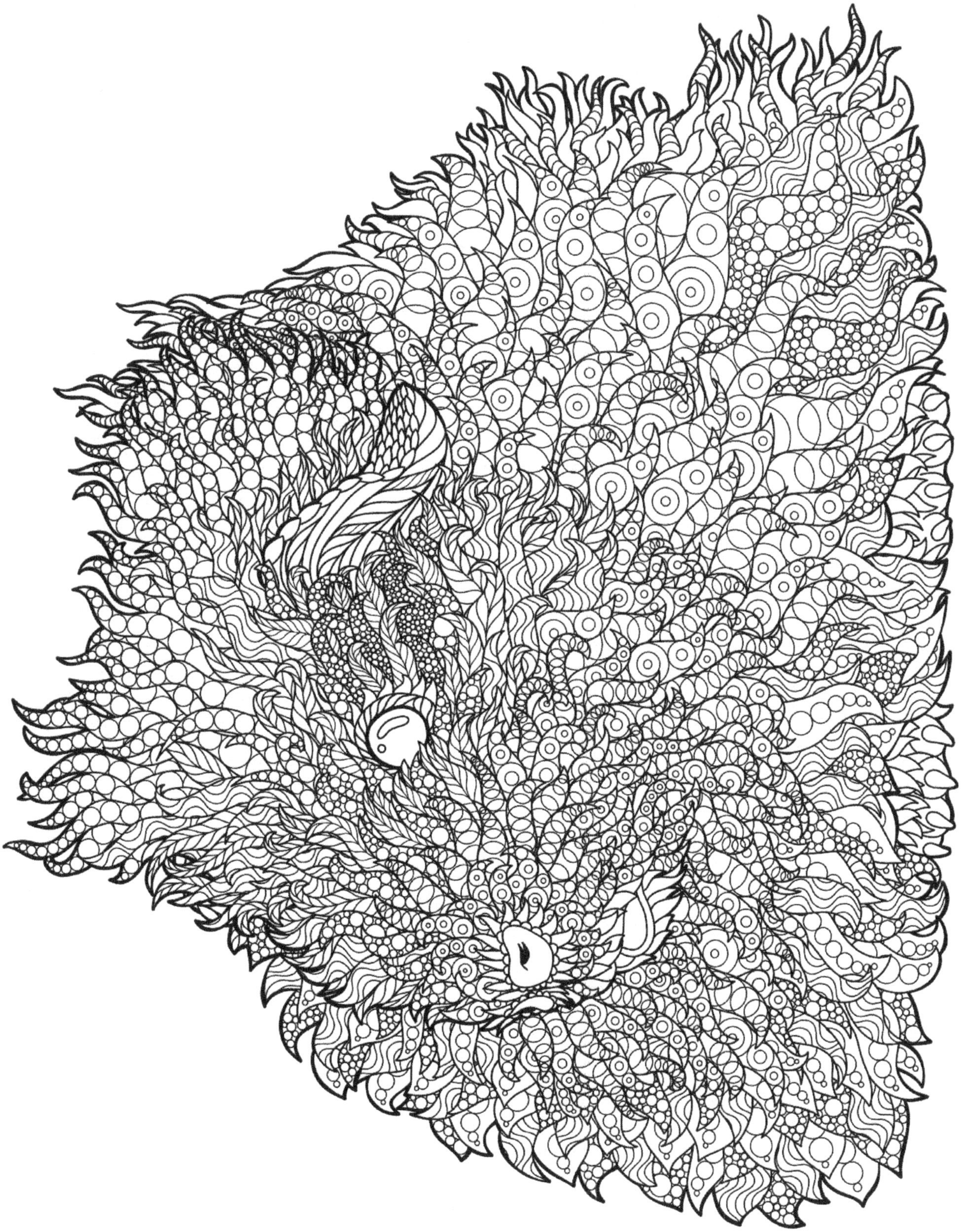

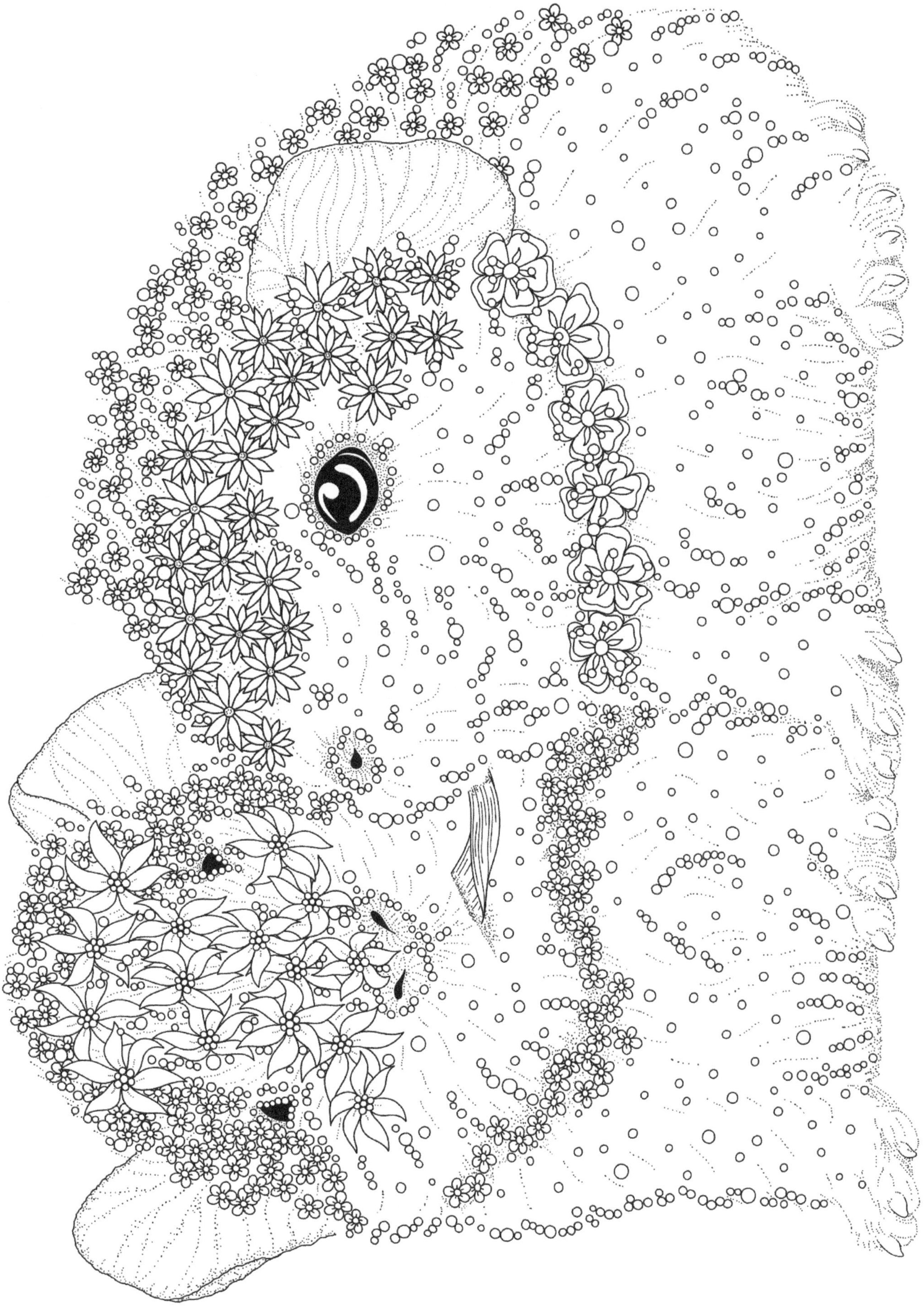

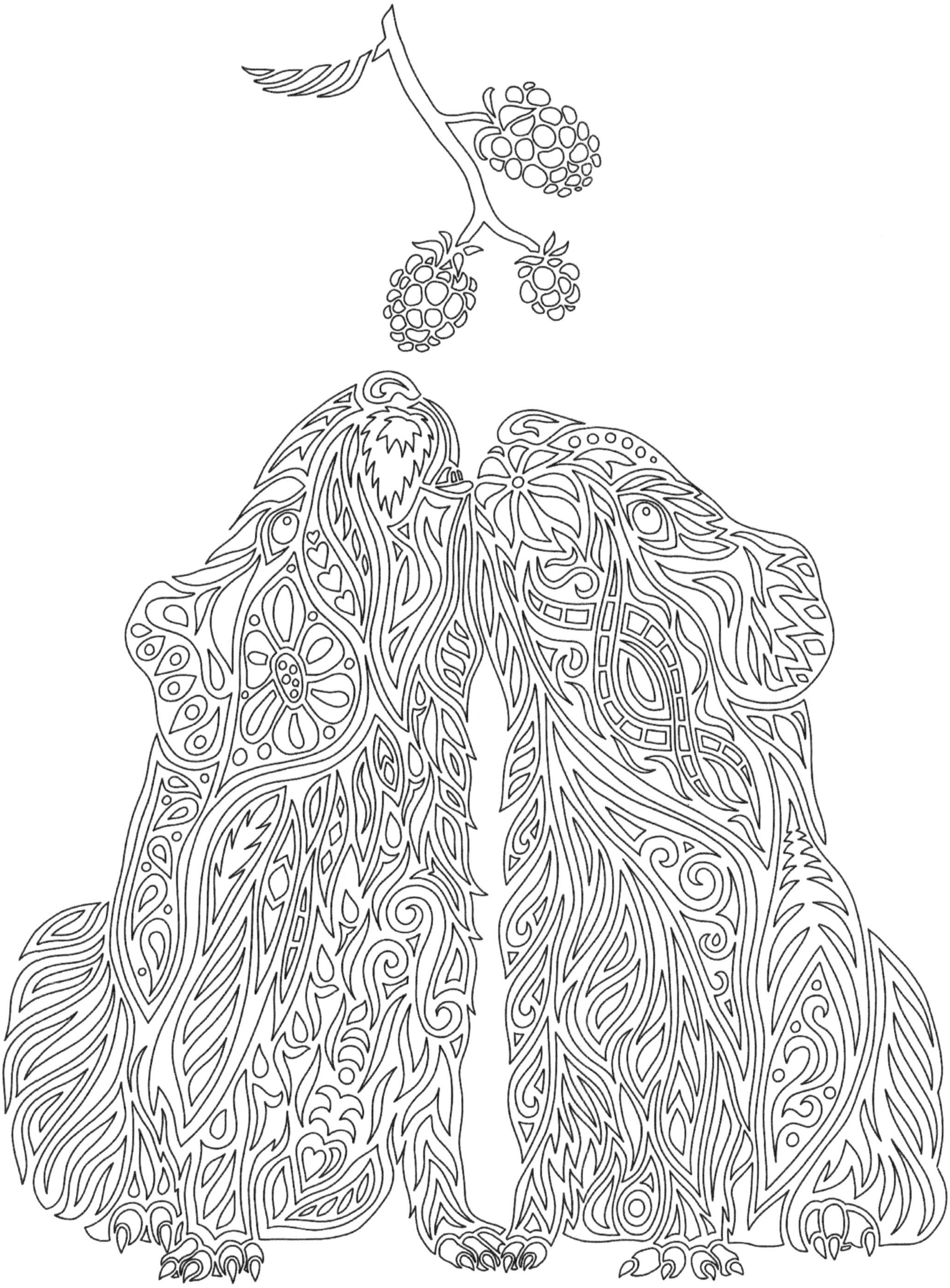

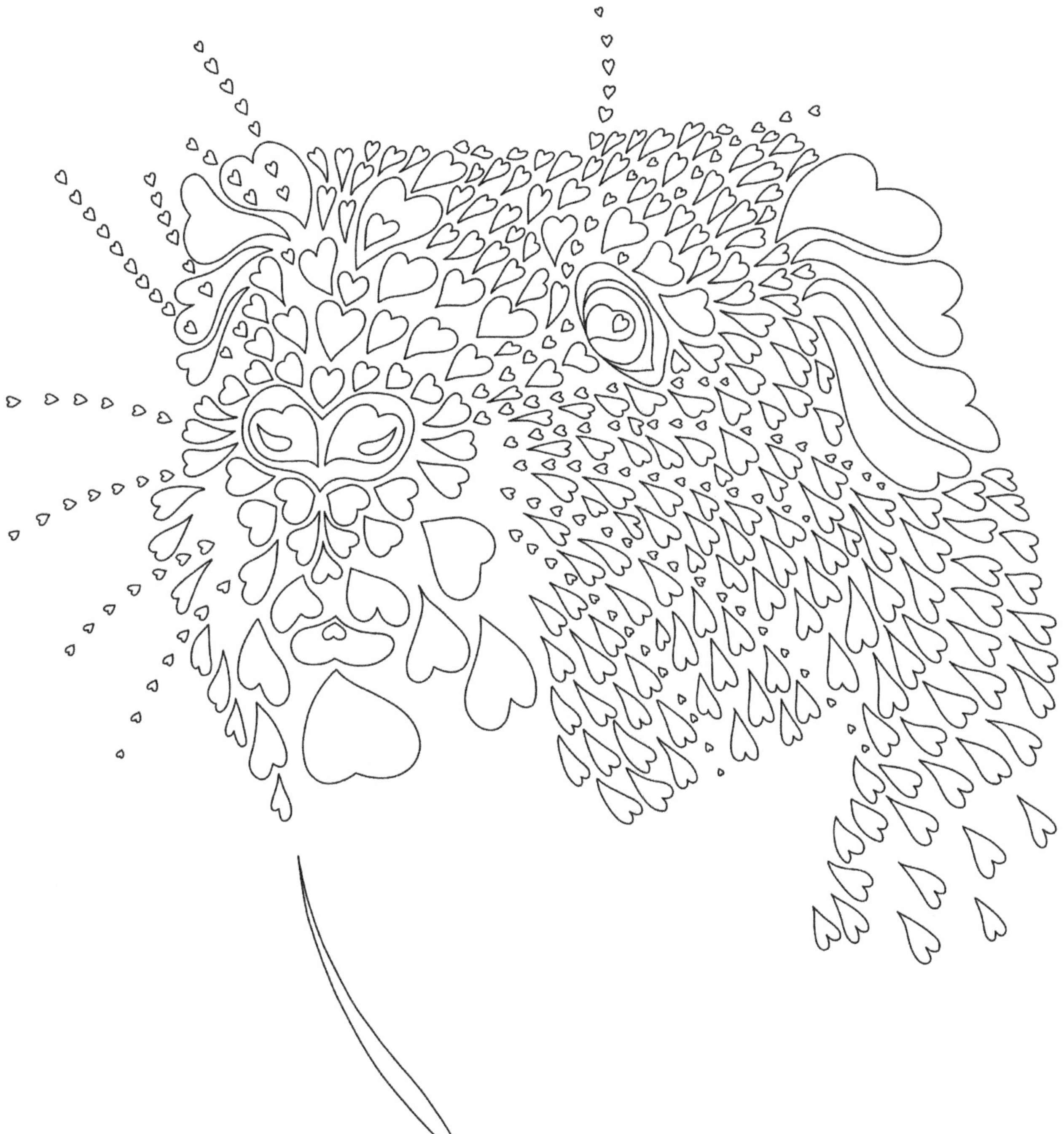

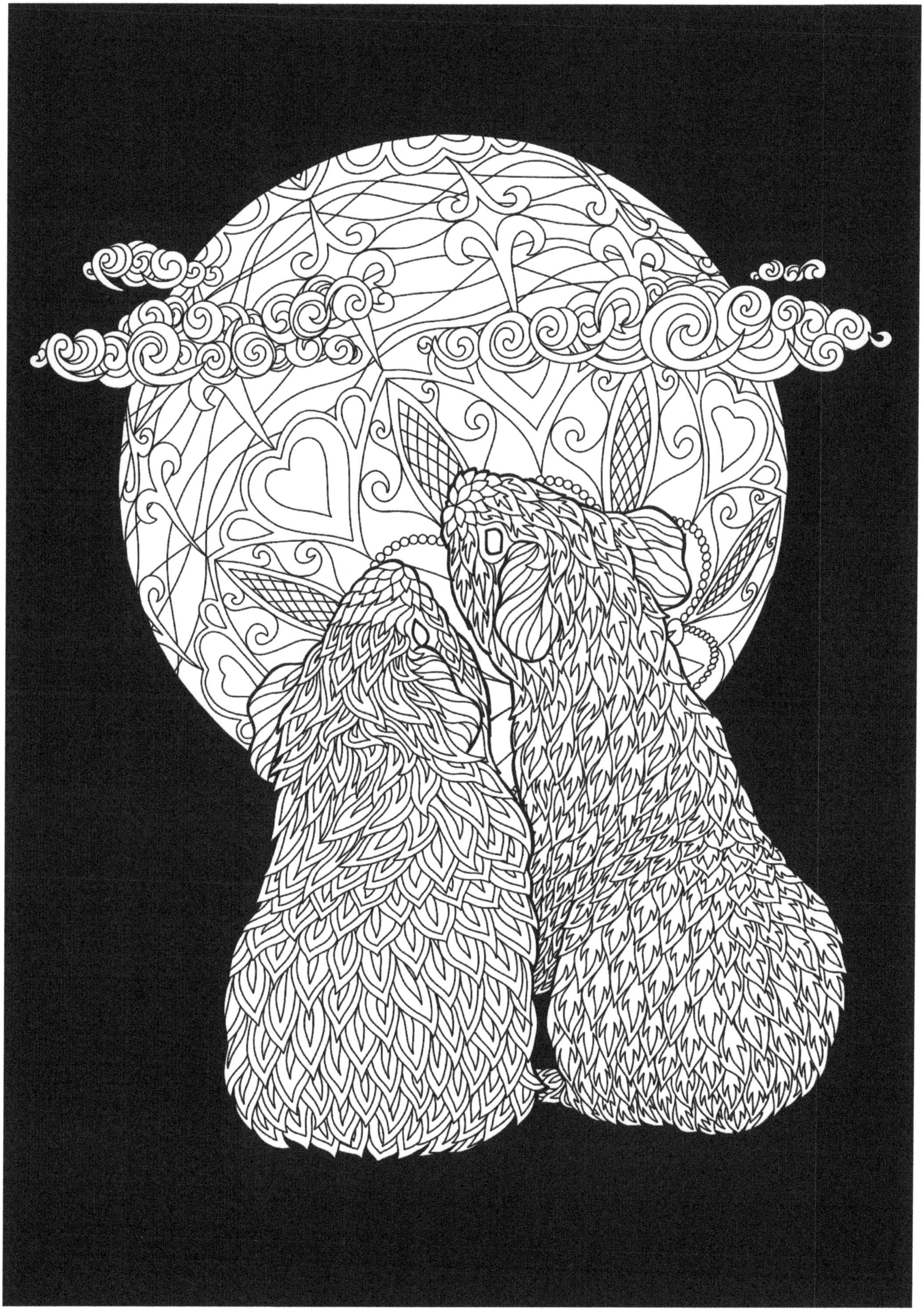

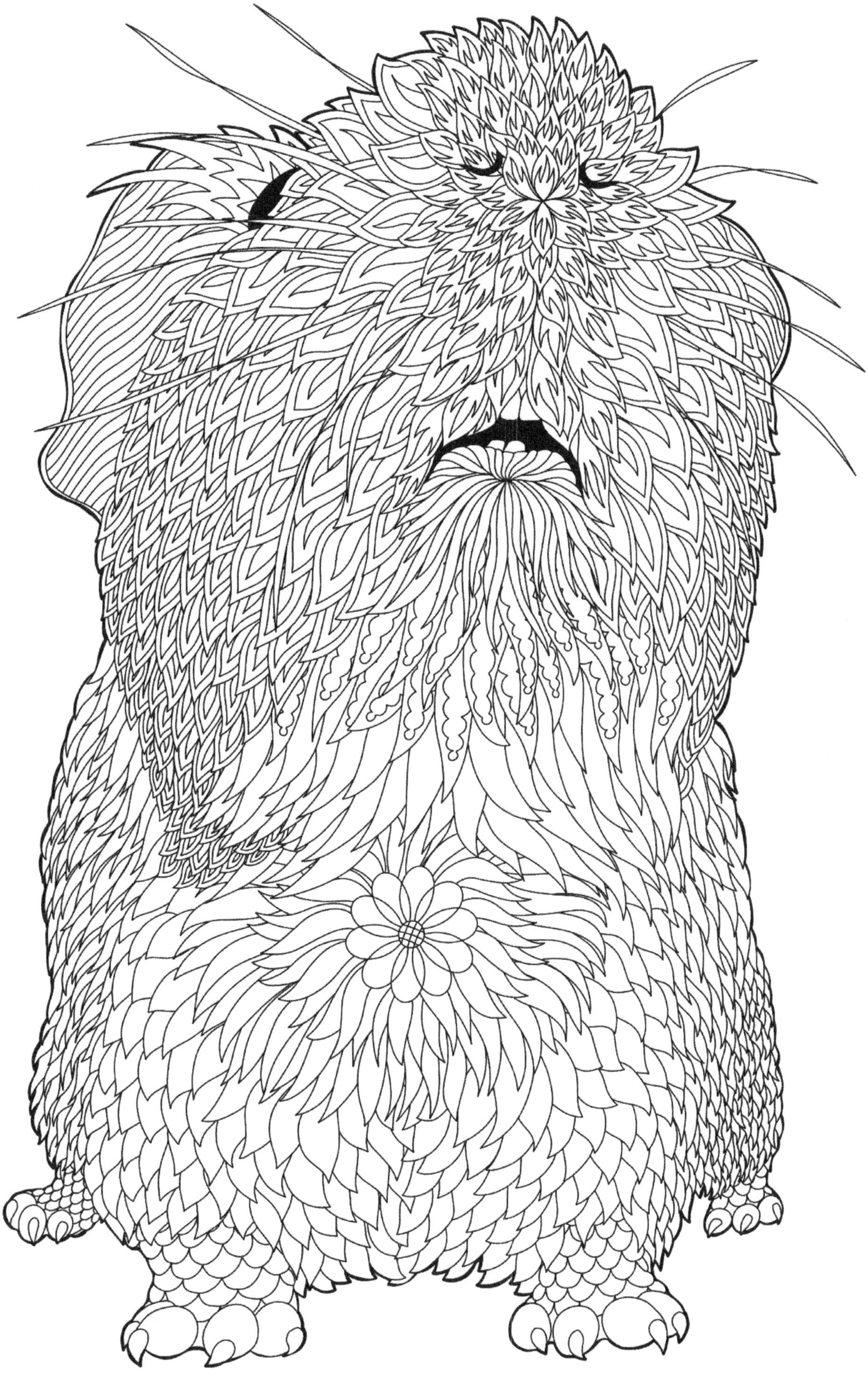

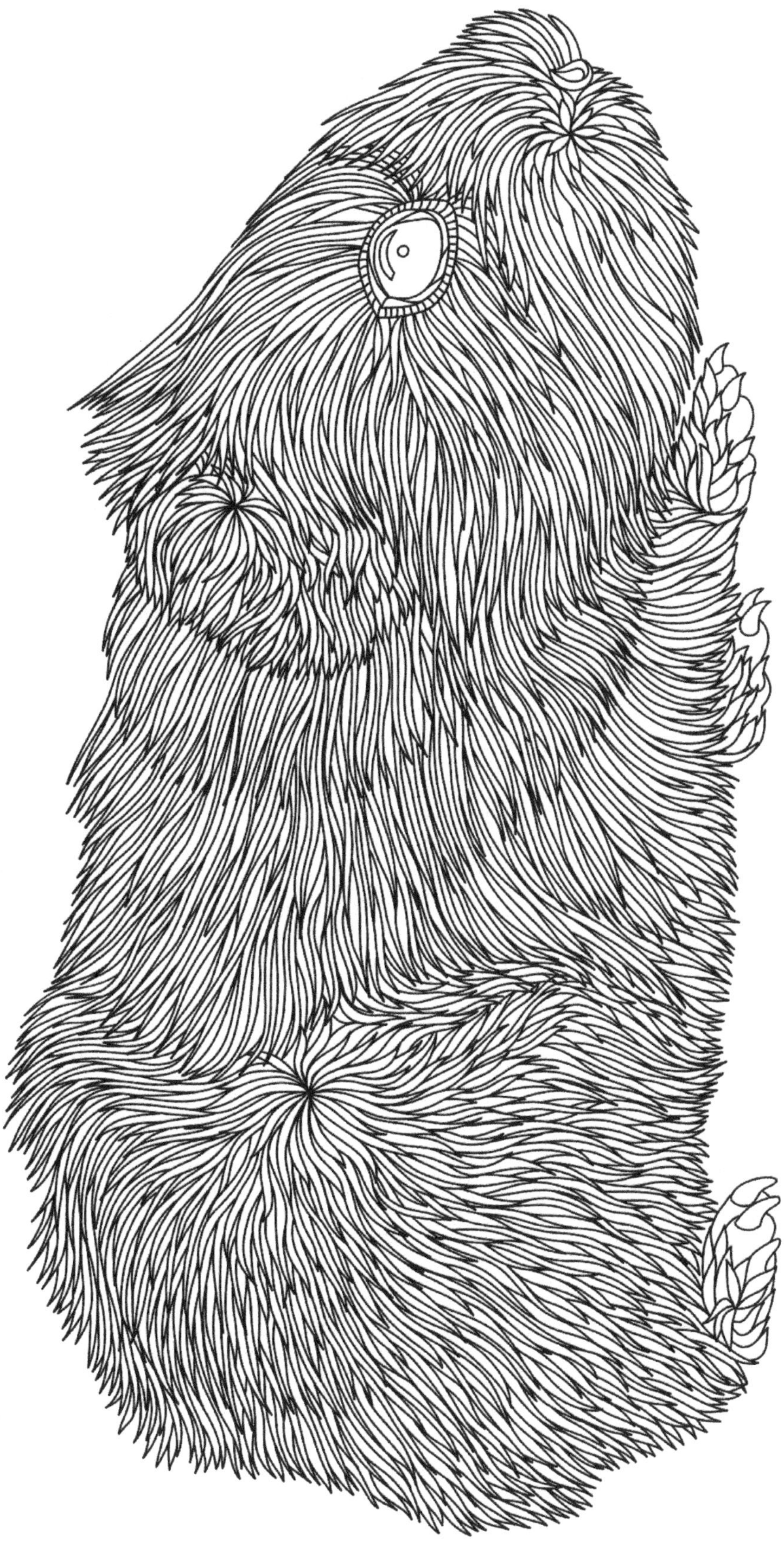

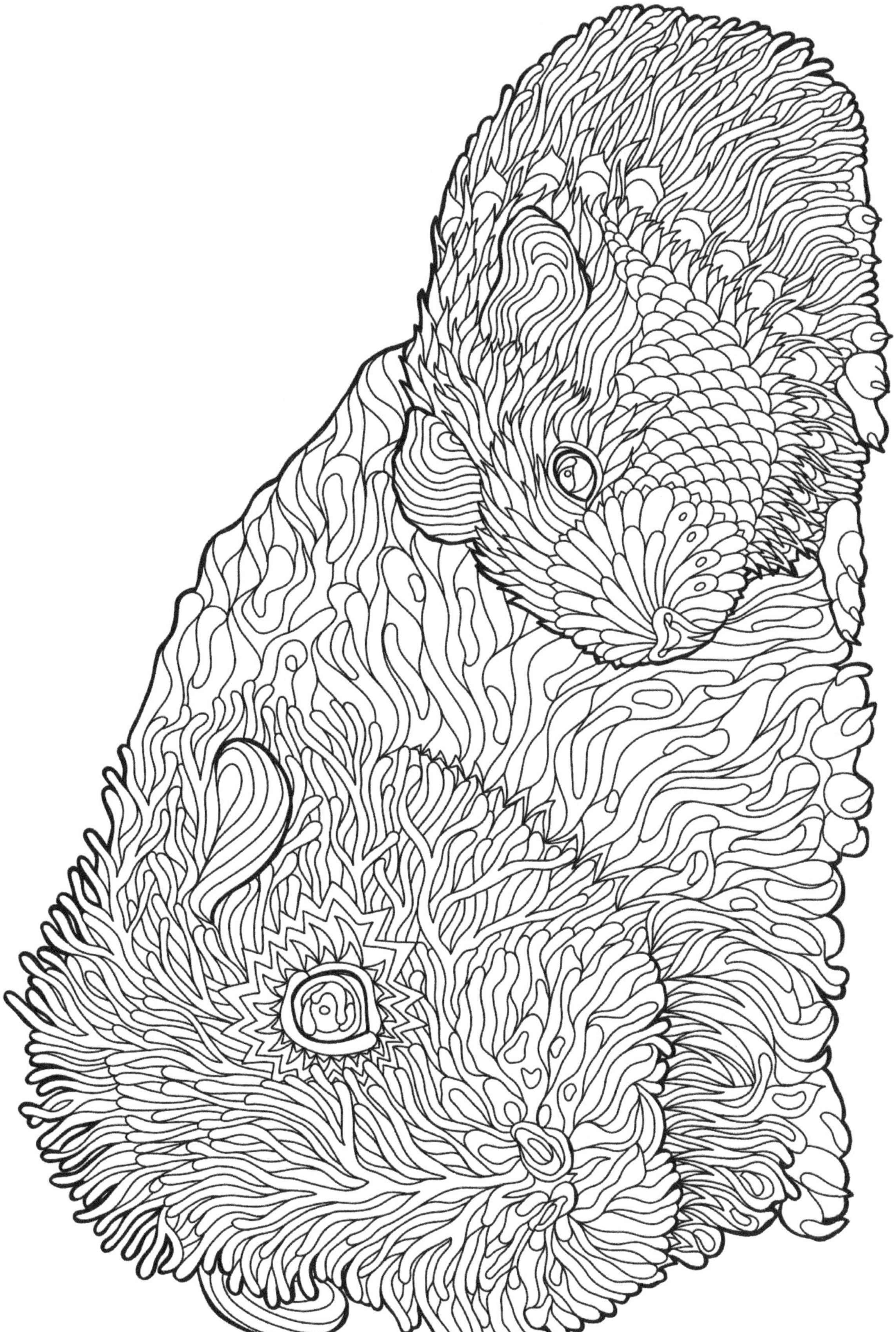

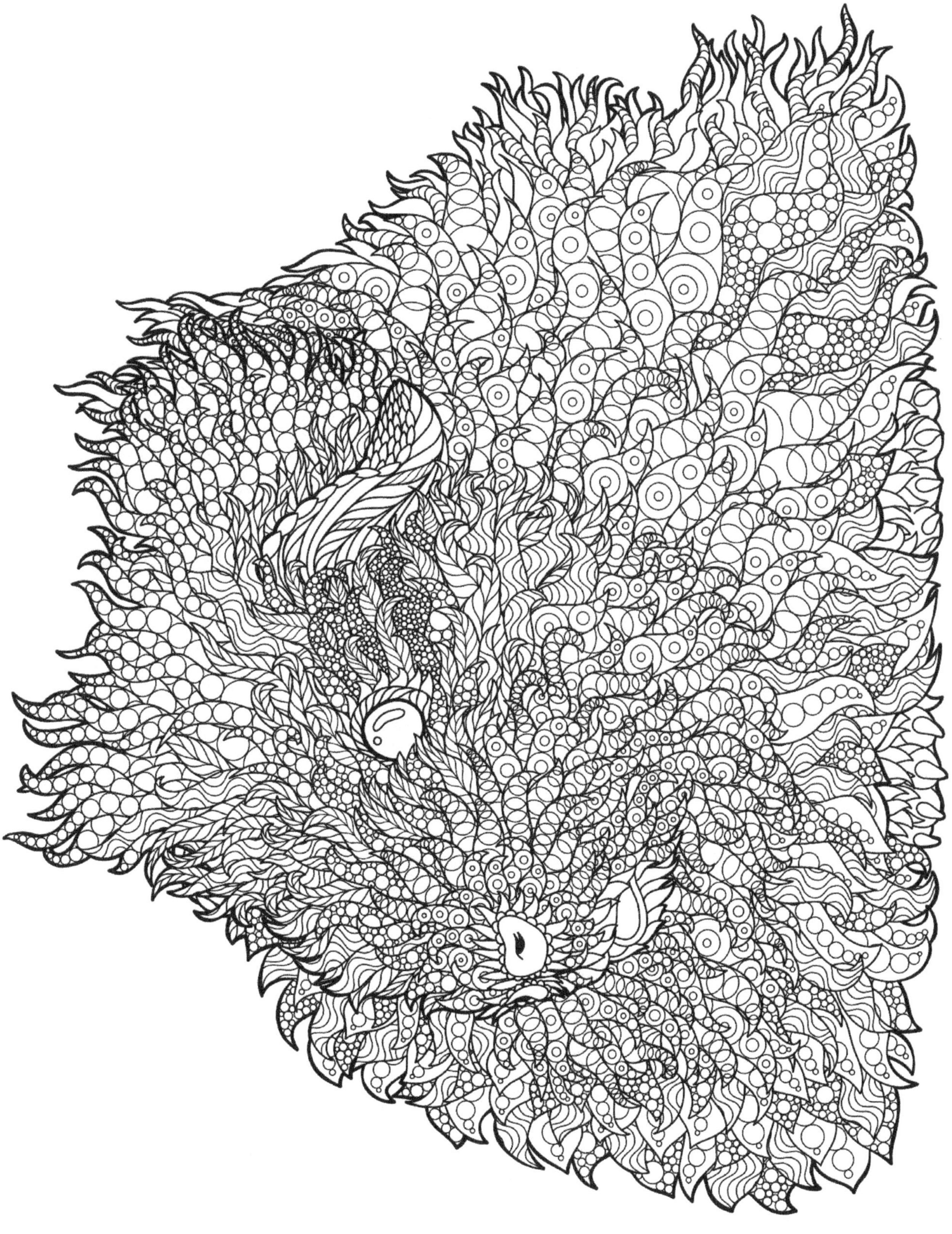

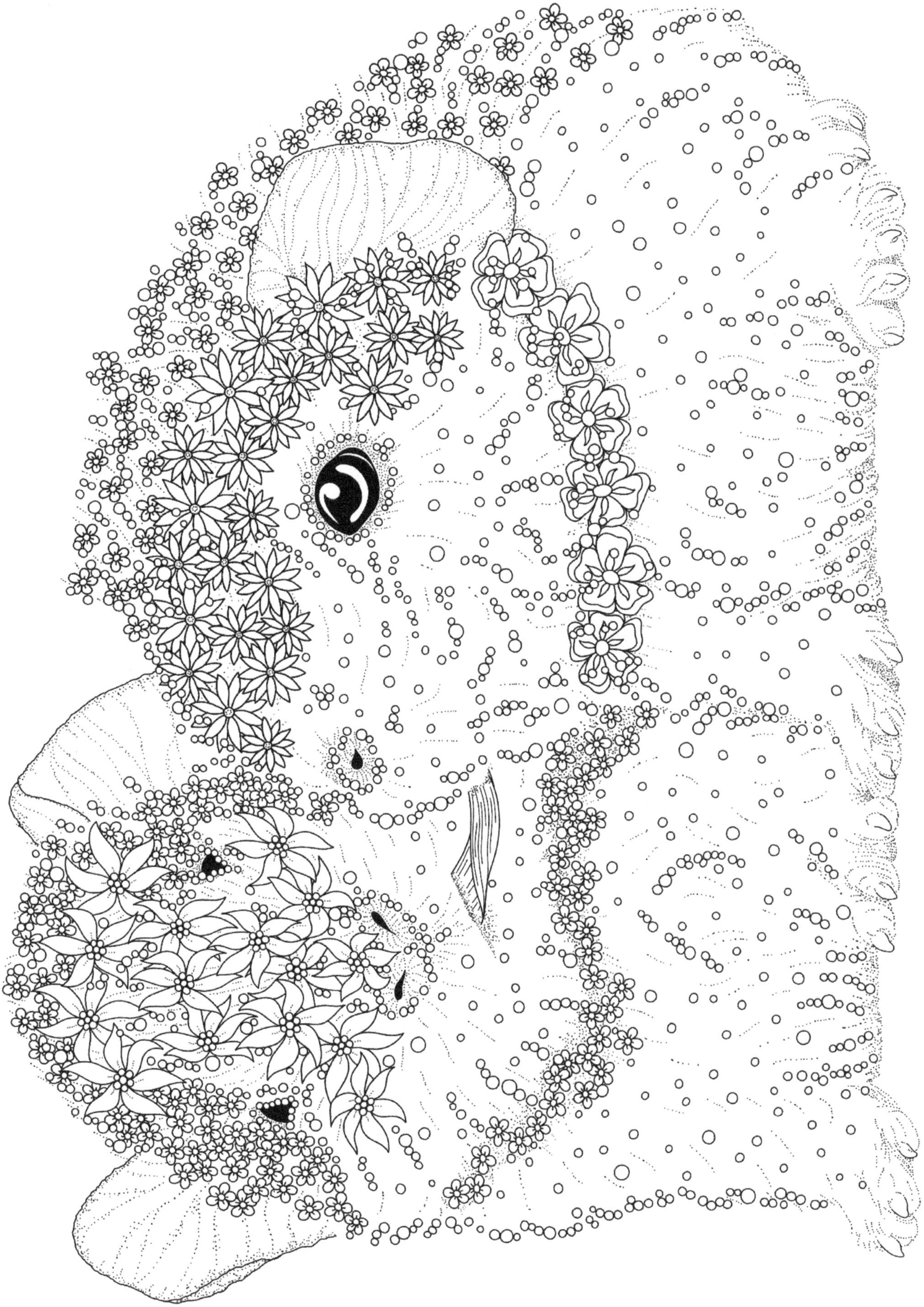

Made in the USA
Coppell, TX
21 March 2022

75278417R00046